Within Shadows

a collection of poems

by Angela Adams

WITHIN SHADOWS
Copyright © 2026 by Angela Adams

All rights reserved. No part of this book may be used or performed without the prior written consent from the author, if living, except in the case of brief quotations embodied in critical articles and reviews.

First Edition
ISBN: 979-8-9948273-0-7

Cover design and interior design by Kalpart
Cover photograph by the author, Iona Abbey, Scotland, 2011.

Published by True Leaves Press
PO Box C, Princeton IL 61356
www.trueleavesbookshop.com
hello@trueleavesbooks.com

Printed in the United States of America

Within Shadows

In Memory of Dr. Emory D. Estes
(1925-2013)

Table of Contents

"Help me tell the truth, you see
That's all I'm trying to do,
Is tell the truth.
I'm not that shy"

-Over the Rhine
from "*Goodbye (This is Not Goodbye)*"

Preface

I wrote the poems in this collection between 1999-2002, after I moved from Florida to Texas.

For a boy.

There's no disguising these are the poems of a 20-year-old coming of age and there's not much social veneer.

Releasing *Within Shadows* now, in a performatively authentic culture, makes me proud of the woman I was then—and the woman I am now.

Angela Adams
Malden, IL
January 2026

"Peanut Ran Away"

Dysfunction whispers through the walls.
Everyone knows there must be something more.
Smile, laugh, pretend to be happy;
Home is where the hate is.

Even the cat knows.

Good kitty.

amen (let it be so)

when young i asked for this:
a stream of consciousness that would cause such inspiration,
to frantically jot fleeting thoughts on napkins in public places
-- catch them! (before you lose your mind) --
with borrowed pens -- yes, i am a poet --
or sometimes eyeliner.
but i did not ask for this:
the disillusionment that accompanies such thought.

oh, again to see the world through veiled eyes --
to believe these people (are.) are not cardboard cutouts,
mere man(nequins) with dubbed over voices.

once i met a boy who intrigued me,
because he held his words hostage inside his mind.
i only spoke to him in cliches,
broken pieces of nothing -- what a shame --
fragments really.
he'll go away in a few days and i've not said more than
"you smoke?"
"yes, i'd say i'm not the average Christian girl"
his eyes pierced my soul
to search for meaning.
maybe i shouldn't care.

i believed in fairy tales, plastic smiles,
"i pledge allegiance to the flag"
life, liberty, the pursuit of happiness, and butterfly wings.
now i'd rather seek than find.
i think he understood.
my fear is i just might be the stereotypical poetic epitome
of my jaded generation,
but maybe then i know more than i give myself credit for.

i have found nothing i can hold
just a tempting hope in One whose smile i've yet to see,
whose soul completes me?
i've resorted to self-medicating:
pills and paper that turn my mind into a black light,
and prophecy -- thus saith the lord.
there was a time when something was sacred,
back when i believed in Forever.
has it ever been more than a melodramatic end to a prayer?
a preface to amen?
(a-men.)

oh, to feel the veil upon this tainted flesh
to touch Forever's skin, to stroke His chest with my fingertips,
to whisper what i want to do to Him -- forever.

i'm the stereotypical poetic epitome
of a jaded generation,
but more and more i feel (my tongue grow) numb
and i see (things that are not real),
as i watch my (plastic) soul melt in the sun.
in a dubbed-over voice i hear myself say
"forever and ever"
"amen"

so pierce me now.
search for meaning.

PSYCH 4430

this boy (who wears his shirt inside out) intrigues me—
the way he sits, the far off look in his eyes.
he wears a plain silver band on his right hand
and writes poetry in class.

get a glimpse of what fills his mind.
excuse me,
mr. inside out boy
can I be your wife?

we could write all day long—
fly on the wings of fleeting thoughts,
to a place where reality is relative to the color of the wind,
where dreams compose our livelihood.

he has red sideburns, carries a shoulder bag
he's always clean.
wearing a plain silver band on his right hand,
the inside out boy intrigues me.

abnormal psychology.

Carlisle Hall

Doors open.
A new girl comes.
Gauges that this ride will be a slow one;
She must anticipate three floors of silence.

As if being examined for disabilities
She quickly says that she has a bad knee,
And if it weren't for twelve flights she'd be taking the stairs
Because this elevator is so slow.

So slow. (And the doors have tried to squish her two days in
a row.)

Smiling, I step back,
Squeezing between a backpack and the metal bar,
Right next to a man with his hands in his pockets,
Next to a girl with her arms folded in front of her breasts like
wings.

The girl with the bad knee is chattering
On and on and on
About how slow this elevator is,
Even though the one in the engineering building is so grand.

I'm stuck with her for three more floors because she's a
philosophy major.

My pants don't have pockets. My jacket has no hood.
My worst fear is not plummeting to my death,
But that two more hurried students will cram in on three and
Force me to listen.

Soup

When mothers fail
And fathers flee,
Children are left to raise themselves.

Days become full of microwave snacks,
Purposely stepping on cracks in big-city sidewalks.
Truth sounds like a lie when
Parents trade birthrights for pittance.

(But I think she turned out pretty damn good.
Yes; pretty damn good, indeed.)

Ohio River Valley

A blanket of haze covers the land,

Smog fills the air;

Calm in the melancholy skies.

Passing the cemetery where many folks stay

I am struck with an eerie sympathy.

Nothing's holding me before these small-town eyes.

Familiar story told by nature,

I come from a long line of leavers.

Envy

When a boy I sang and danced
about the house so free.
When a boy I wrote and thought
within my twilight sea.
When a boy I dreamed of war and fire,
how I hated girls like me.

When a boy I wanted to be a Swiss Army Man,
within my stardream world, confined.
When a boy I worked for naught,
and whiled away the time.

When a boy,
I had love then,
I felt then too.
I used to,
in my prime.

Moloch

In my mind I bow,
kiss the feet of expectation.
Ideals of what should be of
whys and hows

Consume me.

I stand before you
barely clothed.
You try your best
to avert your gaze,
still I know what you see.

So transparent.

Stop pretending
love is dead,
or be a murderer.

Bathing

Holding you tight,
A bottle of wine,
One moment's breath
Between mercurial and divine.
To dive or to dance
In this sea filled with tears,
I humbly grapple with nontheist fears.
I grip your arm,
Pull close to me.
You're Jesus here,
The brink of apostasy.

Evening

The saddest death
is of a dream.
No ceremony,
no burial,
no silk flowers.
No women
in black
praying
the rosaries.

It just dies,
quickly forgotten.

Fahrenheit (Or On Having an Autumn Wedding)

i.

I was born at the end of an era.
We ushered in the generation
Of those holding fears worse than death
(Hypocrisy and lack of love).

While he sleeps my mind races.
I feel too old for this skin,
Unmistakably too young for this experience.
How is it that I am having second thoughts?

Cold feet— attached
To the bottom of the girl
Who has found all she
Ever dreamed of.

ii.

Waiting, I'm patient,
Holding my breath,
Knowing soon you'll arrive.

Console me
With your sweet words,
Your simplest gesture, which speaks of your love.

I would wait my lifetime— and
Perhaps I have,
Perhaps I will.

Expectancy sweetly proceeding
Everything which lets me
Know you are alive.

The hand on my watch skips seconds it seems,
And inside brews the dichotomy
Of anticipation and knowledge.

Once more you come,
As I hoped—
See, I'm learning to grow.

Is this the pattern?
Being a commencement,
Is this to be the end?

iii.
You ask if I'm cold
Because you think you
See me shiver.

Draping your arm around my neck,
Rubbing my shoulders,
I stiffen.

You pause,
As if waiting for me
To say "Warm my feet."

You do, as you say
Love, and whisper those somethings
No one can hear.

My skin breathes and crawls—

Allowing you to touch me

Would it deepen this chill or provide relief?

I walk boldly into winter.

An Empty Page

Distracted nation,
Intoxicated with rage.
Hate provoked to brokenness,
Vice versa,
Etcetera.

Infinite justice to come,
Acts of faith turn into acts of war,
And this is enduring freedom.

You know, I secretly believe
Americans cannot tell
A Muslim from a Hindu,
Just Issac from Ishmael.

Fortresses held captive to fear.
I sit here cold and numb,
Filling an empty page.

Beloved

Hard to describe
what it is that
makes me smile,
Just now.

Feet curling,
fear of falling
off and out—
Yet away
you take me.
I feel like a child,
for laughter is mine.

(How is it that your scent saturates open air
when trees trade their green for winter?
A new love flows through me, as you touch my back,
bringing me to that place where skin melts snow.)

Communication

He wakes quietly; walks gently,
so as not to disturb my sleep.
The perfect gentleman in all things,
commanding respect of me with every breath.
I wonder still why love rests with me,
why in my constant turbulence he remains
the one to brush my hair, protect my dreams.

I, not deserving of such love,
selfish and torn between two worlds.
His strength far beyond me.
Yet, in this, I know my weakness
is covered by his garments,
and that's how it ought to be.

So often I drive him to grasp, to reach
expecting those things of him
that no one can give me.
When he fails, because he will,
he is still my flesh, my love.
He tries.
All I ever say is "I'm sorry."

To the Girl I Once Called Rain

I heard the news.
I smiled for you.
I think of you quite often really,
What with all the violins in the world.

So surely these days are green.

I fear my time has been spent
Making apologies instead of amends.
Life is merely doing what
We wished all those nights.

I know in my haste I missed the day
After tomorrow as it
Turned into the day
Before today,

But here we are.

Everyone's married.

Someone has kids.

No one is left standing,

Wondering how it is that bridges burn

So damn fast,

When somewhere it's

Always raining.

"I like the cello because it's closest to the human voice."
-Amirosh Issa, 2001

Expectation before the first note—
Tuning, octaves, bow patterns,
Fortes and familiar sounds.
The voice of the strings,
Like the human voice.
Yet it can say the same thing, this voice,
Without being redundant.
Somehow there is always variation.
Sounds escape that are vaguely,
Not quite like,
Writing in either cursive or print,
Manic in scope or space.
My mind, longing for arpeggios.
Staccato.
Today feels like a coda,
Life a movement,
Full of broken fifths.

And the Second

Was that third or fifth position?
To reach beyond, within,
Stretching all possible emotion
From a piece of woven wire,
I could never quite get there. . .
Fingers too small for a cello,
Too large for a violin.

(An altogether different environment now,
free use of thought and form—
(stale smell of smoke
on the clothes of those patiently
waiting for class to end)
free from pedagogy, from being
taught from the perspective of how.)

I can't see if your eyes are closed,
But that sounds like treble clef.
My scattered thoughts start
Creeping, walking.
Moving words across empty pages,
They speed with your crescendos.
And that, I think, was seventh.

(On Growing Up in Florida)

A girl with red ringlets stooped to pick up a curious thing.
An egg fallen from a palm tree, the perfect treasure.
It was an act of defiance, a secret wonder,
Being allowed to collect only shells on this day.

She felt the rough egg with her delicate hands.
She held on to it by the loose strands of hair.
Listening to the fluid inside slosh and splash,
As she ran quickly towards her castle.

It was her prize, this egg the tree laid.
Soon it was carefully stashed at the bottom of the bucket
She used to construct turrets and dragon keeps,
Gently covered by sand and seaweed.

Before long, smaller eyes and bigger hands
(Of those acquainted with tree eggs) opened the mystery.
Painted lips partaking, "Go ahead, love, that's milk inside."
Colored fingers delving, "Taste the fruit."

She chewed the egg white, textured like cud,
Then promptly disposed of the tasteless mass.
The inhaled salt numbed her sense of smell,
The egg smelled nothing like Sunday.
Spell of wonder broken, she surrendered her find,
Abandoning the egg and its hoary pulp.
Quietly she walked along the shoreline,
Looking for broken shells.

And she grieved for the cow that climbed the tree.

(On touching the hand of the one called Divine)

A man hung from a tree, that I might not die.
While I walk in silence, He takes pain to His side.
I hear Him crying, the world it divides.
Do I make Him a fool as He calls me His bride?

Known from my birth, yet His love I defy,
Seeking for that which just He can provide.
Groping and clinging to my hold on life,
In all of my doubt, His own death I deny.

Call it the place of the Skull, or a place called Alive,
Brought to a place where I surrender being right,
I see I'm a fool and
I yield Him my life.

Resurrection Sunday

how
beautiful are the feet
of those who
fall at the feet
of the one who
Brings Good News.

how beautiful
are the feet,
beautiful the ground.
how beautiful the blood
that falls at the feet
of the One whose
name I curse,
though Moses couldn't say it.

#1

my heart to His, this crown my cup.
I kneel, He lifts my head.
I drink, I die, my heart to fly,
He stands, I lift my eyes.

to sing, His breath within my lungs,
to speak, His life upon my tongue,
to be, His mantle over me,
to walk is to be free.

my soul to His, this Blood my fate.
I bow, He wipes my tears.
I kiss, I lie, my Lover dies,
He fades, my Spirit sighs.

to see, His light beyond my face,
to know, His truth revealed by grace,
to run, to rise, to live is Christ,
to love is to draw nigh.

my heart to His, I offer up.
I kneel, He lifts my head.
I walk, I die, (my Savior rise)
He stands, I lift my eyes.

to sing, to speak, to know, to see,
to drink His cup for me.
this Blood my fate,
to live is Christ,

for love, I am His bride.

Pockets

One dollar & fifty-eight cents
It's milk money, milk money.
After cashing the checks it's all that's left,
Just money for milk made from beans.
Every roadside stand & greasy pan wants this milk money.
Money for breakfast till Thursday.

One dollar & fifty-eight cents
It's milk money, milk money.
After doing my best it's hard to confess
We've just money for milk made from beans.
Every offering pan & newspaper stand wants this milk money.
Money for missions to Turkey.

One dollar & fifty-eight cents
It's nothing, no thing.
After stopping to rest there's nothing left,
Just money for nothing at all.
Every beautiful hand & school in the land wants milk money.
Money for breakfast till Thursday.

Lust of the Eye, Lust of the Flesh, Boastful Pride of Life

She speaks in cliches and bits of phrases.
Her best thoughts plagiarized
From billboards and bumper stickers,
Proclamations shared by sedans nationwide.

I am a threat to her with my short hair—
An abomination, an aberration, a reminder.
I have it from a good source that once she was like me,
That she dyed her hair and burned her bras.
Now her hair is matted, gray.
Her curves concave.
She will not look a man in the eyes.

A beautiful woman veiled
Because her husband likes tits and ass.

It's Just Too Much, Tonight.

When you're fat you get real good at math.

You calculate how many more people can get on the elevator
without exceeding the weight limit and plummeting to a rapid
sardine-like death.
You calculate the load bearing capacity of wooden staircases.
You quickly add yourself, the car, the passengers, and
even though you know you don't weigh a ton
still, at every bridge, you count.
You add.

When you're fat you tell great jokes.

Even serious words are laden with sarcasm,
allowing others the option of how to hear you.
Left to their own devices, you're quite sure you'd
just be the opinionated fat girl;
so in all things you provide an escape route, an alibi.
You like making people laugh, making them happy;
because laughter gives the illusion that you are.

When you're fat you pay full price.

You buy your clothes in stores that inflate the cost so much
you'd swear they are buying fifty extra yards of material
instead of one,
or that the seamstresses have to undergo cultural training on
obesity.
This gets billed to you in the form of jeans or socks or bras.
You hate going to thrift stores, because they never have your
size.
On the occasion they do, it's because someone lost weight,
and you get their rejects.
Women don't get rid of clothes when they gain weight.

So, when you're fat you own hundreds of shoes.

Shoes to match every dress, every purse, every fancy.
You buy shoes because you don't mind trying them on to see
how they look.
They always fit.
You don't discard shoes because they "make you look fat."
(Who are you kidding, anyway?)
You buy tie-dyed Birkenstocks and flip flops covered with
indoor-outdoor carpet,
or stock up on the latest style.
The shoes will be approved.

When you're fat you get used to being comfortable.

You wear sweats and big shirts every day if you can,
because clothes with waists make one where there is not,
dividing flesh into unnatural hemispheres.
You wear full-seat extra large underwear to conceal
femininity, or none at all to reveal it.
You get used to dumpy clothes because extra large just isn't,
even though you are.
You know it.

When you're fat you get great compliments.

You're constantly made aware of how pretty your face is, how
beautiful your eyes are.
"Is that your natural hair color? It's gorgeous."
"What great shoes!"
Every once in a while you'd like to be a sex object,
while others fight it tooth and nail,
just to know that there are other parts of you that are attractive.
It's comforting to know that some consider fat a fetish.
On days when people think you look particularly good
you are asked if you've lost weight.

When you're fat you shock people.

You surprise them when choosing "fat" to describe someone,
because they are very careful not to say it around you.
Instead, they come up with words like chunky or husky
that describe cookies and dogs better than people.
You shock them when you say you don't have diabetes,
or when you don't make apologies for being who you are.
It's always expected that you're sorry.

When you're fat you die small deaths.

You sacrifice your most dear dreams
on unworthy altars of acceptance.
You walk over your own thresholds.
You take it from behind.
And it's okay.
It has to be.

When you're fat you take your life in jeopardy.

You don't buckle seat belts
because they don't fit.
You don't wear life vests on boats—
hell, you don't even get on boats because you,
and only you,
would cause them to sink.
You'd deserve that.

When you're fat you become creative.

You come up with ways to make people love you,
through education and gifts.
You make the best excuses for staying home at night—
away from crowds where you will be the fattest one.
All of the beautiful people are actors on a stage for you.
You watch, you think.
You write.
Never involved, but always observing.

When you're fat you ask for nothing.

You don't ask for seconds, or raises,

or what you really would like to drink,

because someone will judge, and will decide your fate.

They'll know your secrets.

You ask for nothing, because you are.

Because you're not,

when you're fat.

Mending Wall (Thanks, Bob)

My husband desperately wants to build a fence around our land.
To keep thieves out, to keep dogs in.
He's looking for wood and all I can think about is Robert Frost.

As cliché as it is, I tell him
"Good fences make good neighbors"
For the second time in as many days, and again he nods,
Agreeing with me.

It started out with looking for stain for a fence,
And because of Robert Frost and frozen ground
I am pondering the darkness he moves in.

"And set the wall between us once again
We keep the wall between us as we go."

Portrait

Writing is a vain pursuit.

Chasing metaphors like rabbits over hills and
Into holes best left undiscovered;
Forcing ancient symbols into form.
But a poem is just words.
Just words.

Then Dionysus and Apollo or commodity or social rejection
Come like Christ riding on a white horse,
Convincing me by mere existence of the error of my ways,
The vanity of life, and the truth of pride.

Suddenly, I'm ten years old,
Writing all the way down to aluminum
The trench between there and not,
Using just words to pass notes to my soul or
To find foxholes,
Only to crawl in and remain undetected.

To Matthew

There are volumes in me.
Volumes so long ago shelved,
So long ago stashed in a box,
Locked tight with an impenetrable guard.

Volumes sitting upon the coffee tables,
Upon the token bookcases,
Of those who at best
Consume my memories.

And yet, here you are,
An avid reader, a treasure seeker.
You, who observe the materials this world is made of,
You who care just as much about what and how as why.

You, who delights in finding discarded things
And making them right.
Blowing off the dust with your gentle breath, loosening
Years with your fingertips.

Smooth bristles wetting,
Cleaning the exterior
So that maybe someday another will see
The beauty you know in your mind's eye.

There are pages of fine linen,
Gilded edges darkened by lack of light.
Chapters long forgotten
And never disclosed.

Sentences penned in frantic dreams
Or in the dark of night.
Books waiting for your breath,
Your touch, your insight.

Pages with no need to be read aloud or analyzed,
Just given the attention of a packrat who
Holds onto hidden treasures—
Until they are safe to be seen by the world.

References

Epigraph

Over the Rhine. "Goodbye (This is Not Goodbye)." *Films for Radio*, Back Porch Records, 2001.

"I like the cello because it's closest to

the human voice" - Amirosh Issa; And the Second

These poems were written in 2001 or 2002 during a creative writing class at UTA. Amirosh Issa, a local cellist, played for the class and we wrote poems during his performance.

(On Growing Up in Florida)

During a different session of the same creative writing class, we were given the task of writing a poem based on a one word prompt. Mine was coconut.

Mending Wall (Thanks, Bob)

Frost, Robert. "Mending Wall." *North of Boston*, Henry Holt and Company, 1914.

Acknowledgements

Dr. Emory D. Estes was my favorite professor. As he walked into class, he'd greet us with a hearty "Helloooo, scholars." He nicknamed me "Tiger;" presumably because of my red hair, but maybe because I was so headstrong and intense. My desire to be holy and authentic kept me up at night. One day, I met Dr. Estes for office hours (yes, in Carlisle Hall) and tearfully confessed my conflict. He asked, "Tiger, do you think Christianity has been passed through the ages by idiots?" His question gave me permission to write what was true. To write the words within my shadows of doubt. I submitted an early version of *Within Shadows* as my Honors thesis; Dr. Estes was my advisor. I am ever grateful.

Matthew Adams was the boy. We will celebrate 27 years of mostly-happy marriage in October 2026. Ahab im kol libi.

About the Author

Angela Adams returned to the Midwest in 2007 after spending her formative years in Florida and Texas. Angela holds a BA in English and Writing from the University of Texas at Arlington and an MA in Theology from Bethany Theological Seminary. When she's not working her day job in tech, you can find her at True Leaves Bookshop (the indie bookshop she and her husband, Matthew, founded in 2023) or at home with her two remarkable teens and many well-loved pets.

www.ingramcontent.com/pod-product-compliance
Lightning Source LLC
Chambersburg PA
CBHW031241130726
47988CB00008B/3180